What Causes Sexual Orientation? Genetics, Biology, Psychology

The Gallup's Guide to Modern Gay, Lesbian, & Transgender Lifestyle

BEING GAY, STAYING HEALTHY

COMING OUT:
TELLING FAMILY AND FRIENDS

FEELING WRONG IN YOUR OWN BODY:
UNDERSTANDING WHAT IT MEANS TO BE TRANSGENDER

GAY AND LESBIAN ROLE MODELS

GAY BELIEVERS:
HOMOSEXUALITY AND RELIGION

GAY ISSUES AND POLITICS:
MARRIAGE, THE MILITARY, & WORK PLACE DISCRIMINATION

GAYS AND MENTAL HEALTH:
FIGHTING DEPRESSION, SAYING NO TO SUICIDE

HOMOPHOBIA:
FROM SOCIAL STIGMA TO HATE CRIMES

HOMOSEXUALITY AROUND THE WORLD:
SAFE HAVENS, CULTURAL CHALLENGES

A NEW GENERATION OF HOMOSEXUALITY:
MODERN TRENDS IN GAY & LESBIAN COMMUNITIES

SMASHING THE STEREOTYPES:
WHAT DOES IT MEAN TO BE GAY,
LESBIAN, BISEXUAL, OR TRANSGENDER?

STATISTICAL TIMELINE AND OVERVIEW OF GAY LIFE

WHAT CAUSES SEXUAL ORIENTATION?
GENETICS, BIOLOGY, PSYCHOLOGY

GAY PEOPLE OF COLOR:
FACING PREJUDICES, FORGING IDENTITIES

GAY CHARACTERS IN THEATER, MOVIES, AND TELEVISION:
NEW ROLES, NEW ATTITUDES

What Causes Sexual Orientation? Genetics, Biology, Psychology

by Bill Palmer

Mason Crest Publishers

MASON CREST PUBLISHERS INC.
370 Reed Road
Broomall, Pennsylvania 19008
(866)MCP-BOOK (toll free)
www.masoncrest.com

First Printing
9 8 7 6 5 4 3 2 1

Library of Congress Cataloging-in-Publication Data
Palmer, Bill, 1957-
What causes sexual orientation? : genetics, biology, psychology / by Bill Palmer.
    p. cm. -- (The Gallup's guide to modern gay, lesbian & transgender lifestyle)
ISBN 978-1-4222-1757-3 (hardcover)   ISBN 978-1-4222-1758-0 (series)
ISBN 978-1-4222-1876-1 (pbk.)   ISBN 978-1-4222-1863-1 (pbk series)
1. Homosexuality—Juvenile literature. 2. Sexual orientation—Juvenile literature.
3. Sex (Biology) I. Title.
HQ76.26.P353 2011
306.76'6—dc22
                            2010021830

Produced by Harding House Publishing Service, Inc.
www.hardinghousepages.com
Interior design by MK Bassett-Harvey.
Cover design by Torque Advertising + Design.
Printed in the USA by Bang Printing.

PICTURE CREDITS

Contents

INTRODUCTION   6

1. GENDER, GENDER IDENTITY, AND SEXUAL ORIENTATION   9

2. BORN GAY: BIOLOGICAL THEORIES OF HOMOSEXUALITY   24

3. BECOMING GAY: PSYCHOLOGICAL THEORIES OF HOMOSEXUALITY   35

4. WHY DOES IT MATTER?   49

BIBLIOGRAPHY   61

INDEX   62

ABOUT THE AUTHOR AND THE CONSULTANT   64

Introduction

We are both individuals and community members. Our differences define individuality; our commonalities create a community. Some differences, like the ability to run swiftly or to speak confidently, can make an individual stand out in a way that is viewed as beneficial by a community, while the group may frown upon others. Some of those differences may be difficult to hide (like skin color or physical disability), while others can be hidden (like religious views or sexual orientation). Moreover, what some communities or cultures deem as desirable differences, like thinness, is a negative quality in other contemporary communities. This is certainly the case with sexual orientation and gender identity, as explained in *Homosexuality Around the World*, one of the volumes in this book series.

Often, there is a tension between the individual (individual rights) and the community (common good). This is easily visible in everyday matters like the right to own land versus the common good of building roads. These cases sometimes result in community controversy and often are adjudicated by the courts.

An even more basic right than property ownership, however, is one's gender and sexuality. Does the right of gender expression trump the concerns and fears of a community or a family or a school? *Feeling Wrong in Your Own Body*, as the author of that volume suggests, means confronting, in the most personal way, the tension between individuality and community. And, while a community, family, and school have the right (and obligation) to protect its children, does the notion of property rights extend to controlling young adults' choice as to how they express themselves in terms of gender or sexuality?

Changes in how a community (or a majority of the community) thinks about an individual right or responsibility often precedes changes in the law enacted by legislatures or decided by courts. And for these changes to occur, individuals (sometimes working in small groups) often defied popular opinion, political pressure, or religious beliefs. Some of these trends are discussed in *A New Generation of Homosexuality*. Every generation (including yours!) stands on the accomplishments of our ancestors and in *Gay and Lesbian Role Models* you'll be reading about some of them.

One of the most pernicious aspects of discrimination on the basis of sexual orientation is that "homosexuality" is a stigma that can be hidden (see the volume about *Homophobia*). While some of my generation (I was your age in the early 1960s) think that life is so much easier being "queer" in the age of the Internet, Gay-Straight Alliances, and Ellen, in reality, being different in areas where difference matters is *always* difficult. Coming Out, as described in the volume of the same title, is always challenging—for both those who choose to come out and for the friends and family they trust with what was once a hidden truth. Being healthy means being honest—at least to yourself. Having supportive friends and family is most important, as explained in *Being Gay, Staying Healthy*.

Sometimes we create our own "families"—persons bound together by love and identity but not by name or bloodline. This is quite common in gay communities today as it was several generations ago. Forming families or small communities based on rejection by the larger community can also be a double-edged sword. While these can be positive, they may also turn into prisons of conformity. Does being lesbian, for example, mean everyone has short hair, hates men, and drives (or rides on) a motorcycle? *What Does It Mean to Be Gay, Lesbian, Bisexual, or Transgender?* "smashes" these and other stereotypes.

Another common misconception is that "all gay people are alike"—a classic example of a stereotypical statement. We may be drawn together because of a common prejudice or oppression, but we should not forfeit our individuality for the sake of the safety of a common identity, which is one of the challenges shown in *Gay People of Color: Facing Prejudices, Forging Identities*.

Coming out to who *you* are is just as important as having a group or "family" within which to safely come out. Becoming knowledgeable about these issues (through the books in this series and the other resources to which they will lead), feeling good about yourself, behaving safely, actively listening to others *and* to your inner spirit—all this will allow you to fulfill your promise and potential.

James T. Sears, PhD
Consultant

chapter 1

Gender, Gender Identity, and Sexual Orientation

Are people born homosexual? Do experiences early in a person's life turn him gay? What causes homosexuality?

Before we can begin any discussion of these questions, we have some important words and *concepts* we need to understand. And maybe we ought to start with a very basic one: What exactly do we mean by "homosexuality"?

The word "homosexuality" itself is made up of a Greek word, *homo*, which means "same," and *sexuality*, which comes from the ancient Latin language and means a person being either female or male. So very simply, "homosexuality" means "same sex." The word was unknown before the mid-1800s, but it quickly took on its modern definition: the emotional and physical

What's That Mean?

Concepts are general ideas about the how and why of things.

attraction of a person of one sex (male or female) for people of the same sex—males who are attracted to males, and females who are attracted to females. "Gay" is a less scientific word, but it's the one many homosexual people prefer to call themselves.

Like everyone else, people who are gay started out as babies. There they were—the next generation, behind a glass window in the hospital nursery. There were big babies, little babies, pink babies, brown babies, babies of all descriptions; some crying, some sleeping, and some getting their first look at the world around them, each one of them a unique individual from the moment she was born. But in one

Even though these babies have just been born, the people around them have already begun making assumptions about who they are based on whether they are a boy or a girl.

important way there seems to be only two kinds of babies in the nursery, and you can tell just from looking at the babies which ones are which: the baby boys wear little blue caps, and the little girl wear little pink caps.

Blue for boys and pink for girls are the traditional colors of *gender* identification. This identification is made in the delivery room (or often even earlier through ultrasound pictures of the baby before it's born) by a quick glimpse of the baby's *genitalia*. "It's a boy!" or "It's a girl!" are often the first words a new mother hears when her baby is born. This simplest form of sex identification, the visual one, is the outward appearance of *biological* sex that is determined at the moment of conception, when the father's sperm fertilizes the mother's egg. That first complete cell has either an XX *chromosome*, in which case it will grow into a girl baby, or an XY chromosome. (It's a boy!)

What's That Mean?

Gender refers to a person's identity, whether masculine or feminine.

The scientific term for the male's penis and testicles and the female's vagina is *genitalia*.

Biological refers to the physical characteristics of living things that can be studied by scientists (called biologists).

A *chromosome* is a microscopic thread of genes within a cell that carries all the information that determines what a person looks like, including sex.

From the time they are very young, babies are often dressed according to traditional gender roles. The person this baby girl grows up to be may have nothing to do with the frilly pink outfit she is wearing here, however.

Gender, then, is a basic biological ***trait***, since both sexes are necessary for ***reproduction***. Throughout the animal kingdom, mature males produce sperm cells to fertilize the egg cells produced by mature females. And the new life produced at conception grows and matures in the female's body. As you know, that's where the babies came from that we just visited in the hospital nursery!

From the moment they are born, little girls and little boys are expected to be different

What's That Mean?

A *trait* is a characteristic of an individual, such as eye color or gender.

Sexual *reproduction* is the method by which human beings produce children: the male's sperm fertilizing the female's egg and the new life developing in the female's body.

from each other. What is considered to be normal male or female behavior is different in different places around the world, and it has been different at different times in history, but we all know the basics. Females are expected

to be gentler and more emotional and sensitive. They are caregivers and nurturers. They like to dress up as princesses and play with dolls when they are little, and they grow up liking "pretty" things. Males are rougher and tougher; they don't cry easily. Boys like competitive sports and getting dirty, and they grow up wanting to be big and strong. Parents, teachers, and other authority figures almost always have different expectations for how boys and girls will act, and boys and girls are often rewarded for behaving in these gender *appropriate* ways. "Boys will be boys," as the saying goes. And boys who don't act like boys are made fun of for being "sissies," while girls who like to play rough games are called "tomboys."

Some of these traits that we so easily assign to males and females may really be as basic as biology. As we know, each sex has a different role in reproduction and in family life, and for much of the time human beings have been on Earth, these roles have shaped gender differences, just as they do in

What's That Mean?

other animal species. Men are usually bigger and stronger in order to hunt for food for their wives and their young ones and to protect them from danger. Women are usually smaller than men, much of their physical energy concentrated on reproduction. For untold thousands of years, women had to be cared for by their husbands and their community while they were pregnant and caring for their babies; women spent much of their lives taking care of their children and staying close to the homes they kept for their husbands and families. Many of the basic *gender roles* that seem so natural to most of us are the result of a long history of behaviors determined by the basic reproductive needs of our species.

For many people, probably the majority, these gender roles are reasonably comfortable. While many of these roles are changing as women have gained greater gender equality, and both men and women today have more freedom to behave outside the stricter sex roles of the past, our species still needs people who are happy to fulfill their biological roles as mothers or fathers—and our culture still needs to support those roles. But as powerful as biology

EXTRA INFO

Sometimes it is hard to understand exactly what is meant by the term "gender," and how it differs from the closely related term "sex." "Sex" refers to the biological and physiological characteristics that define men and women. "Gender" refers to the socially constructed roles, behaviors, activities, and attributes that a given society considers appropriate for men and women. To put it another way, "male" and "female" are sex categories, while "masculine" and "feminine" are gender categories. Aspects of sex will not vary much between different human societies, while aspects of gender may vary greatly.

Here are some examples of sex characteristics:

- Women menstruate, while men do not.
- Men have testicles, while women do not.
- Women have developed breasts that are usually capable of producing milk, while men do not.
- Men generally have larger, thicker bones than women.

Some examples of gender characteristics :

- In the United States (and most other countries), women are responsible for housework (even if they also have jobs outside the home).
- In many countries, women wear dresses, but men do not.
- In some countries, men drive cars, while women do not.
- In some cultures, women cry easily and openly, but men do not.

(Adapted from the World Health Organization, www.who.int/gender/whatisgender/en/)

A person's idea of himself or herself as either a female or a male, no matter which biological sex they were born, is their *gender identity*.

Sexual orientation is a person's physical and emotional attraction to the opposite sex (heterosexuality), the same sex (homosexuality), or both sexes (bisexuality).

LGBT stands for lesbian, gay, bisexual, and transgender. It's an inclusive term that covers all four groups of people.

and gender roles are, human beings are a lot more complicated than that.

Transgender

A person's biological sex is not necessarily the same thing as their *gender identity* or their *sexual orientation*. According to the Human Rights Campaign, the largest *LGBT* political organization in the world, up to 1 percent of the adult population does not feel comfortable with the gender roles and the physical sexual traits of the sex with which they were born. These people are referred to as transgender, and growing up transgender can be a very challenging experience.

"I just never felt comfortable in my own body," explains Marty, a transgender male who was born and raised a female. "I was forced to wear dresses and do all kinds of 'girl' things—but as far back as I remember, I knew I was a boy. I just knew it."

In India and Pakistan, hijiras are usually biological males who have taken on a female gender identity. Although accepted as a part of society in the traditional past, hijiras were declared to be criminals in the nineteenth century and today still struggle against prejudice and discrimination.

EXTRA INFO

As many as one in every thousand babies is born with either external genitalia or internal sexual organs that are not clearly either female or male. These people are known as "intersex." In the past, doctors often made a decision—sometimes even without the parent's permission—to perform surgery to "normalize" an intersex child, even though it might not have been clear which gender the child might grow up to be. Sometimes people who have been "assigned" a male or female gender early in life, either by surgery or by a decision by their doctors and parents, grow up with serious gender confusion and identity problems. The Intersex Society of North America is an organization that educates doctors and parents about intersex issues and assists intersex people in dealing with the challenges of their medical condition. Many intersex people live happy and satisfying lives outside of the "normal" female and male gender identity.

Marty was always attracted to male gender roles and "boy" stuff, like competitive sports and building things with tools.

"I started living as a man full time when I got out of the military, and I started on male **hormones** when I was twenty-five. I can't tell you how thrilled I was when my beard started to grow in. And my therapist and my transgender support group were with me every step of the way."

Besides taking hormones, some transgender people undergo sexual re-assignment surgery, which can be a long and very expensive series of operations. They may also go through the process of legally changing their names and gender in official records.

Lili Elbe was one of the first people to have sexual reassignment surgery. Born male in Denmark in 1882, she travelled to Germany in 1930 for a series of experimental surgeries. She died in 1931 from complications from her fifth surgery, a uterus transplant that she hoped would allow her to have children.

Marty has had his first two surgeries toward becoming the biological male he believes he always was, and he is saving his money for his next operation. (Most health insurance companies will not cover re-assignment procedures.)

"I've had to give up a lot," says Marty. "Some of my family members still won't accept that I'm not 'Martha,' and I've lost friends because I'm transgender. But I am who I am. I'm not trapped in the wrong body anymore."

Issues of gender and sexual orientation are rarely as simple and clear cut as people would like to make them.

Homosexual

Much more common than transgender people are homosexuals, people whose sexual orientation is toward their own gender rather than the opposite sex. While the figures vary a lot depending on what studies you go by, as many as one in ten people (about the same percentage of the population that is left handed) are gay.

The reason why the majority of people in the world are heterosexual (sexually attracted to people of the other, or opposite, gender) is really pretty obvious. As we talked about earlier, for most of human history, females and males have had to have a physical sexual relationship in order to produce the next generation of babies and keep the human species going. The attraction to members of the opposite sex comes "naturally" for most people. But why does a sizeable minority of human beings have a sexual orientation—homosexuality—that seems to have nothing to do with making babies? The "why" of homosexuality is definitely not so obvious.

Trying to answer the question "what causes homosexuality?" is part of a major **debate** in science that has been going on for many years. It's the debate over "nature versus nurture." The "nature" side of the debate would be supported if it could prove that gay people are born gay, that being gay is a biological trait like the color of a person's skin. The nurture side says that being gay is the result of the way a person is raised, his relationship with his parents, and his environment; he wasn't born gay, in other words, but he became gay. Or could it be, as some people believe, that certain people simply make a choice to be gay? Nature, nurture, or choice?—as we shall see, the answers to the question aren't completely clear. But the issues these questions raise are very important to the LGBT community's continuing struggle for full *civil rights* and acceptance. They are also a part of every person's—straight or gay— desire to understand themselves and who they are.

Find Out More on the Internet

Gender Identity
gayteens.about.com/od/glbtbasicsforteens/f/whatisgenderid.htm

Gender Roles in Society
www.buzzle.com/articles/gender-roles-in-society.html

Read More About It

Abate, Michelle Ann. *Tomboys: A Literary and Cultural History.* Philadelphia, Penn.: Temple University Press, 2008.

Pascoe, C. J. *Dude, You're A Fag: Masculinity and Sexuality in High School.* Berkeley, Calif.: University of California Press, 2007.

chapter 2

Born Gay: Biological Theories of Homosexuality

Are gay people born gay? Is there a homosexual *gene*? Is there a basic biological reason why some people are attracted to members of their own sex? Are gay people biologically "different" from straight people? Research on these questions has been going on for many years, mostly by scientists on the "nature" side of the nature-versus-nurture debate.

Genetics is the study of the inheritance of biological traits, the passing on of physical and other *inborn* characteristics from parents to their children through the process of sexual reproduction. How does it work?

A Quick Lesson in Genetics

The basic building blocks of genetics are genes, carried on microscopic strands of genetic material called chromosomes. These chromosomes, twenty-three contained in the male's sperm and twenty-three in the female's egg, come together in unique combinations when the sperm fertilizes the egg in a process called conception. A child's biological parents each contribute exactly half of the genes that carry all the new baby's potential biological characteristics. The way these genes combine, which is unique in every conception

What's That Mean?

A *gene* is a microscopic sequence of DNA located within a chromosome, which determines a particular biological characteristic.

Those traits, whether they're visible or not, that are a part of who we are at birth are called *inborn*.

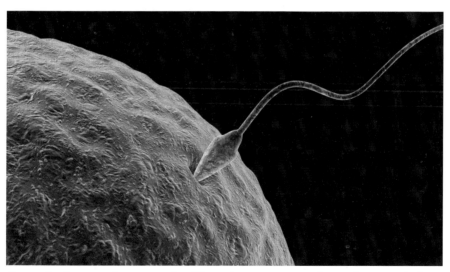

From the instant the sperm fertilizes the egg, some of our characteristics have already been determined.

(except in identical twins, as we shall see) determines which particular biological traits the baby will inherit from its parents.

Full biological brothers and sisters have access to the same genetic material from their parents, but because of the way the parents' chromosomes divide in half for the sperm and egg cells, their genes can combine together in nearly infinite ways. This means that brothers and sisters will share some traits and have others that are very different from each other. However, because identical twins develop from a single fertilized egg (and the same combination of the same forty-six chromosomes) they are genetically identical. If there is a gay gene, or a combination

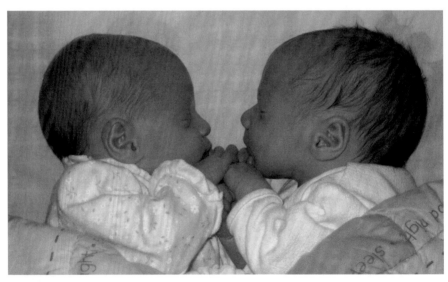

While twins can share many of the same traits, they may also be very different. Traits are caused by a variety of factors, including genetics and environment.

of genes that causes homosexuality, identical twins should always share the same sexual orientation. That's why studies of twins have been of great interest to scientists.

Genetics and Homosexuality

A major study in 1991 by psychologist Michael Bailey from Northwestern University and psychiatrist Richard Pillard from the Boston University School of Medicine found that if one male identical twin was gay, there was a 52 percent chance that the other twin would be too. In the case of fraternal (nonidentical) twins, if one twin was gay there was a 27 percent chance that the other twin was also gay. A similarly large-scale study of lesbian twins had similar results (48 percent for identical twins, 16 percent for fraternal twins). If we go by the accepted estimate that there's a one-in-ten chance that a *random* individual in the population is gay, these percentages are five times the expected rate for identical twins and double the expected rate for fraternal twins. Other twin studies have supported these findings.

What's That Mean?

A *random* individual is one picked out of a group for no particular reason.

Scientists have also looked at how many gay people are in extended families. The results of some of these studies have found that homosexuality seems to be more common in some families than in others and that there is a possibility that people inherit their "gay genes" from their mother's (the maternal) side of the family, since a gay person's maternal cousins are more likely to be gay than would be expected in a random sample of family members.

While these twin and family studies are far from **conclusive**, they do strongly suggest that there is at least some, and probably a significant, genetic influence on homosexuality.

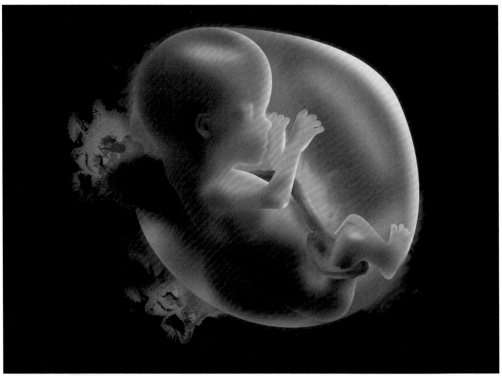

Before babies are born, their mothers' hormone levels can affect their development.

Prenatal Influences

But even if being homosexual is not a genetic trait—and no specifically gay gene has yet been found—there are other biological *theories* about what makes people gay, theories that look at what goes on inside a mother's body during the nine months that her baby is developing. *Prenatal* sex hormone levels may differ at significant times during a woman's pregnancy, her health and her environment may affect the development

of the baby, and certain genes are known to "turn on" or "turn off" for unknown reasons. The reason scientists have looked for a prenatal cause for homosexuality is the fact that some studies have shown certain other biological traits, traits that seem to be unrelated to sexual preference, are more common in gay people than in the straight population. Here are a few results from these trait studies:

- Left-handedness is one-third more common (31%) in gay men and twice as common among lesbians (91%) than among straight people.

- The left half of the brain is larger than the right in the majority of gay men and heterosexual women, while the right half is larger in lesbians and heterosexual men.
- Gay men tend to score higher than straight men in tests of language ability, while lesbians score similarly to heterosexual men, and higher than straight women, in spatial ability (the understanding of objects in physical space).

EXTRA INFO

Homosexuality may not be about making babies the way heterosexuality is, but it appears as a normal part of sexual behavior throughout the animal kingdom. Homosexuality has been observed in close to 1,500 species and is well-documented in over 500, including black swans, mallard ducks, and penguins, as well as all the apes, elephants, giraffes, sheep, hyenas, lizards, and even fruit flies! It is sometimes a show of dominance of one male over another, but it is usually simply friendly and playful. Eight percent of sheep show a homosexual preference, and same-sex penguin pairs mate for life and sometimes even raise orphaned chicks together. Researcher Petter Bøckman has written, "No species has been found in which homosexual behavior has not been shown to exist, with the exception of species that never have sex at all, such as sea urchins." While some anti-gay people say that homosexuality is a "crime against nature," nature seems to feel differently!

Some male penguins have been discovered to prefer the company of other males, and in fact, have remained together as mates for life.

- The index and ring fingers of gay men and heterosexual women tend to be the same length, while in straight men and lesbians the index finger is usually longer.

These studies are also far from conclusive, but some of these findings (brain size and finger length, for example) may be related to the levels of male hormones to which the developing baby is exposed.

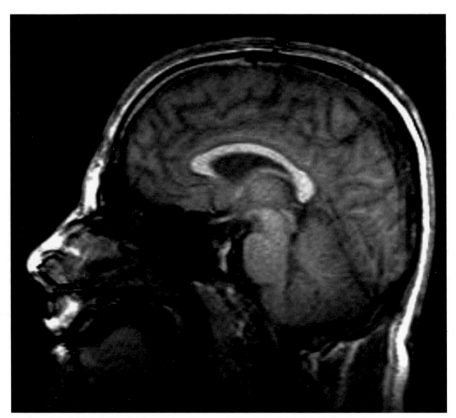

Some scientists think the structure of the brain has a lot to do with a person's sexual orientation.

Developing female babies exposed to high levels of male hormones at a certain time during their mother's pregnancy may be more likely to become lesbians, and male babies exposed to lower levels may be more likely to be gay men when they grow up.

Born Gay

But it's not as simple as gay men being more like heterosexual women and lesbians more like heterosexual men. Early experiments where gay men were given large doses of male hormones in order to make them more "manly" were a failure. High levels of male hormones simply increased the sex drive of these men, a sex drive still directed toward other men, making them, in a sense, *more* gay rather than *less* gay!

So, twin studies, family studies, and research on physical traits common to gay people all seem to strongly indicate—but maybe not prove—a biological cause for homosexuality. Dr. Qazi Rahman, a lecturer in biology at the University of London who has been involved in the brain size study we looked at, says of his research, "As far as I'm concerned there is no argument any more—if you are gay, you are born gay."

Find Out More on the Internet

Gay Twin Studies
gaylife.about.com/b/2007/08/03/gay-twins.htm

Left-Handedness and Gay People
www.narth.com/docs/lefthand.html

Was Lady Gaga Born Gay?
blog.taragana.com/e/2010/03/24/was-lady-gaga-born-gay-102290

Read More About It

LeVay, Simon. *The Sexual Brain*. Cambridge, Mass.: MIT Press, 2004.

Robinson, T. R. *Genetics for Dummies, Second Edition*. New York: John Wiley & Sons, 2010.

chapter 3

Becoming Gay: Psychological Theories of Homosexuality

The "nurture" side of the debate about what causes homosexuality brings us to the very *complex* science of the human mind and human behavior called psychology. For many years, *psychologists* and *psychiatrists* have studied how sexual preference may be more a matter of mind than of biology.

Homosexuality as a "Mental Disorder"

The scientific study of the human mind is only a little over a hundred years old. One of its famous founders, the Austrian psychiatrist

What's That Mean?

Something that is *complex* is complicated and not easy to understand.

Psychologists and *psychiatrists* both study the human mind and human behavior, but psychiatrists are medical doctors, while psychologists are not.

Sigmund Freud (1856–1939) believed that all human beings were basically bisexual and that a person's adult sexual orientation, whether heterosexual or homosexual, was largely the result of his or her early childhood experiences. But while Freud believed that homosexuality was just a variety of normal human sexual behavior, it took many years before the science he helped establish caught up with his **progressive** ideas.

For much of the twentieth century, most psychologists and psychiatrists classified homosexuality as a serious mental illness and considered homosexuals to be sick and abnormal. Medical science supported the church and the legal system in the **oppression** of gay and lesbian people. Homosexuals were not only sinners and criminals, they were sick, too. Gay people were committed to mental hospitals by the thousands and subjected to "treatments" that included being shot up with drugs and hormones, electroshock, and even brain surgery. Subject to this kind of treatment and the victims of prejudice and rejection, is it any wonder gay people were being described by doctors as lonely, unhappy, and often suicidal?

What's That Mean?

Progressive ideas are those that support human freedom and progress.

Oppression is a system of social and legal prejudice that keeps a certain group of people in an inferior position.

As recently as the middle of the twentieth century, homosexuals could be committed to psychiatric hospitals, like Bellevue in New York City, seen here. Not until 1973 did the American Psychiatric Association remove homosexuality from its list of mental disorders.

Thousands of gay men and women underwent years of long, psychologically painful therapy with doctors who told them they were deeply sick and could never live happy, fulfilling lives unless they were totally dedicated to being "cured." In *Cures: A Gay Man's Odyssey*, the historian and gay activist Martin Duberman tells a sadly typical story of deep frustration with the psychiatric profession in the 1950s as he sought help in dealing with his homosexuality.

The bad old days of gay people and the mental health profession started to improve in the 1960s and, at a historic meeting in 1973, the American Psychiatric Association (APA) removed homosexuality as a mental **disorder** from the APA's *Diagnostic and Statistical Manual of Mental Disorders* (DSM-II) in response to pressure both within and outside the APA from the newly organized gay liberation movement.

EXTRA INFO

Even more than thirty years later, a minority of mental health professionals still continue to see homosexuality as an abnormal condition that can be "cured." Reparative therapy programs, that is, therapy to "repair" a person's sexual preferences, is still supported by some religious organizations and still promises unhappy gay and lesbian people a "normal," heterosexual lifestyle despite strong evidence that it doesn't work.

Most gays and lesbians have made their peace with the mental health profession that was once part of a system that oppressed and misunderstood them. In fact, many thousands of gay and lesbian people work in the mental health field today, and many gay people, like many straight people, have had positive, supportive experiences in therapy.

But even if homosexuality is no longer considered a "mental disorder" by most of the scientific community, the reason *why* a certain percentage of people (perhaps as many as one in ten) are gay continues to interest researchers in human behavior. And old *stereotypes* die hard, even for scientists.

Homosexuality and Gender

As we discussed already, biological gender, gender identity, and sexual orientation are really separate issues in human behavior. But most research on the psychological causes of homosexuality has focused on the gender identity of gay people. The *assumption* of this research is that women who are sexually attracted to other women must somehow be, at least on some level, psychologically *male* and that no man would be attracted to other men unless at least a part of him was *female*.

One of the most widely accepted psychological theories of what causes homosexuality has to do with how parents relate to their child

What's That Mean?

A *disorder* is a mental or physical disease.

Stereotypes are ways of thinking about people not based on who they are but on the expected behavior of the group they belong to.

An *assumption* is an often-weak idea upon which other ideas are based.

early in life. In 1962, the psychiatrist Irving Bieber published an extremely **influential** research study titled *Homosexuality: A Psychoanalytic Study of Male Homosexuals*, based on the results of a 500-item questionnaire completed by 107 gay men and 100 heterosexual men. Dr. Bieber concluded that the vast majority of the homosexual men in his study were raised by close-binding, over-protective mothers who discouraged their sons' masculinity and kept them from having a healthy relationship with their fathers, siblings, and peers. And even more significant to his future homosexuality, according to Dr. Bieber, was a boy's relationship with his father:

> The father-son relationship . . . revealed uniformly an absence of loving, warm, constructive paternal attitudes and behavior. In my long experience, I have not found a single case where, in the developing years, a father had a kind, affectionate, and constructive relationship with the son who becomes homosexual. This has been an unvarying finding. It is my view, and I have so stated and written, that if a father has a kind, affectionate, and constructive

What's That Mean?

Something or someone that has a lot of power to affect what people think is *influential*.

relationship with his son, he will not produce a homosexual son, no matter what the mother is like.

Dr. Bieber believed that a boy's relationship with his father was the main factor in whether or not he was a homosexual. Later evidence disproved this theory, however.

This "over-protective mother/distant father" theory of homosexuality was widely accepted as fact, despite the small size of the sample (107 men, all of whom were in therapy to "cure" their homosexuality) until the APA took homosexuality off its mental disorder list in 1972. The theory continues to influence many people, however, both professionals and nonprofessionals, and their understanding of the psychological "why" of homosexuality.

A related theory has been called "the sissy boy syndrome," after a book published by the psychiatrist Richard Green in 1987, *The Sissy Boy Syndrome: The Development of Homosexuality*. Based on the Ameri-

The toys a child enjoys playing with have nothing to do with his sexual orientation.

can Psychiatric Association's addition to the 1980 edition of the *Diagnostic and Statistical Manual Of Mental Disorders* (DSM-III) of what is called Gender Disorder in Childhood, children who are diagnosed with this syndrome have a "strong cross-gender identification" and extreme discomfort with their "normal" gender roles. More specifically, the manual states that this discomfort can be seen in a boy's lack of interest in "rough and tumble play" or a rejection of typical male toys. For girls, this discomfort can be observed in her "rejection of urinating in the sitting position" or her expressing the desire not to grow breasts or begin menstruating. This disorder, according to the DSM-III, can be observed in children as young as two or three.

In his very influential book, Dr. Green presented the results of a fifteen-year study on the development of homosexuality. In the conclusion of the book, he states plainly that the majority of boys who exhibit feminine characteristics in everyday behavior will "grow up" to be homosexual. And according to Dr. Green, boys who are "sissies" and girls who are "tomboys" can only be "cured" of their future homosexuality by a serious *intervention* by their parents and mental health professionals—by constant training to behave

What's That Mean?

An *intervention* is an organized effort to help or change someone.

EXTRA INFO

At their 2009 meeting, the American Psychological Association declared that mental health professionals should not tell gay clients they can become straight through therapy or other treatments. In a resolution adopted by the association's governing council in a 125-to-4 vote, the association issued a rejection of what is called reparative therapy, a treatment practiced by a small but vocal group of therapists, often religious conservatives, who maintain that gay men and lesbians can change. No solid evidence exists that such change is likely, says the resolution. The association said some research suggested that efforts to produce change could be harmful, causing depression and suicidal thoughts. Instead of seeking such change, the association urged therapists to consider multiple options, which could include celibacy and switching churches, for helping clients live spiritually rewarding lives in instances where their sexual orientation and religious faith are in conflict. The association has criticized reparative therapy in the past, but a six-member panel added weight to that position by examining eighty-three studies on sexual orientation change conducted since 1960.

in gender-appropriate ways combined with years of therapy. Dr. Green and others like him have claimed success in preventing gender disordered children from growing up gay.

Peterson Toscano participated in the ex-gay movement for seventeen years before coming out as a gay man. He is now active in the LGBT community, speaking out against the ex-gay movement, as well as encouraging the LGBT community to do more to support people of faith within their community.

Becoming Gay: Psychological Theories of Homosexuality   45

Interacting Causes

But in the last twenty years, gay people themselves and the majority of scientists have been rejecting these theories as **simplistic**. As gay and lesbian people have come out in large numbers, they have come to understand—and have been teaching their straight friends and families—that the tired old stereotypes of sissy men who were "too close" to their mothers and women "who want to be men" do not represent the diversity of the gay community or the real-life experiences of many gays and lesbians. To put it simply, too many gay men were not "sissy boys" and did have strong, positive relationships with their fathers, while too many gay women had no gender-role conflicts as little girls. (And on the flip side, **effeminate** men were often happily heterosexual, and many "tomboy" little girls grew up to be women who enjoyed doing active, stereotypically "boyish" things while being enthusiastically attracted to the opposite sex.)

Out and proud gay people in the twenty-first century have had the opportunity to reject the roles of "girly men" and "manly women" that are still powerful stereotypes of gay people. Or maybe even more

People have a lot of stereotypes about what LGBT people look and act like. Some stereotypes might fit a certain person at a certain time, but most aren't true for everyone, or even for most. And really, does it matter?

important, the gay community has been able to accept the gender role diversity of some of its members. What's *wrong* with being a "sissy boy," and why would parents want to train a child *not* to be whom he is and who he was meant to be?

There is no clear psychological explanation of why some people are homosexual. Early life experiences and family relationships may have an effect on sexual orientation, but human behavior is so much a combination of mind and brain—the psychological and the biological working together—that it is nearly impossible to separate them. And the real question is: why does it matter what causes homosexuality?

Find Out More on the Internet

Gender Identity Disorder in Childhood
www.narth.com/docs/fitz.html

Facts About Homosexuality and Mental Health
psychology.ucdavis.edu/rainbow/html/facts_mental_health.html

Read More About It

Duberman, Martin. *Cures: A Gay Man's Odyssey, Tenth Anniversary Edition*. Boulder, Col.: Westview Press, 2002.

Savin-Williams, Ritch C. *The New Gay Teenager*. Cambridge, Mass.: Harvard University Press, 2005.

chapter 4

Why Does It Matter?

Nature or nurture? Genetics, biology, or psychology? It doesn't seem as if there are any absolutely clear answers as to what causes homosexuality. And while some people outside the gay community want to argue that being gay is a choice, we can quickly eliminate that particular "cause" simply by asking gay people why they think they are gay. Many, perhaps most, gay people knew that they were "different" at a very young age, many long before they had even heard the word "gay." Most gay people believe they were born gay, because their "gay-ness" is such a basic and natural part of who they are; other gay people believe they "became" gay early in life, but very few gay people can even imagine what it would mean to "choose" to be homosexual. Do people choose to be heterosexual? One thing does seems clear, a person's sexual orientation is as basic to who he is as the color of his eyes (and you didn't chose your eye color either).

On November 15, 2008, eleven days after Prop 8 was passed in California, limiting marriage to heterosexual couples, approximately one million people held protests across the country, calling for it to be repealed.

So why does it matter what causes homosexuality, any more than it matters what causes heterosexuality?

Through the political efforts of gay people themselves and with the help of their progressive-thinking *allies*, the gay community has come a long way in recent years toward acceptance in society with full legal and civil rights. But the struggle continues, and gay people will always remain a minority group within the majority

What's That Mean?

Allies are people on the same side and who support the same things.

population. While one of the most important respon-
sibilities of government in a free society is to protect
the rights of minority groups from oppression by the
majority, gay people still do not have the same rights
to marry, to be protected from being fired from their
jobs because of their sexual preference, or to serve
openly in the military, all rights that straight people
take for granted. Gay people are still in a position,
unlike any other minority group in America, where
rights legally granted to them by the courts can be
taken away from them by the vote of the majority.

EXTRA INFO

The California Supreme Court ruled on May 15, 2008 that same-
sex couples have the right to marry in California. But Proposition
8, which legally limits marriage to one man and one woman, was
approved by a majority of voters less than six months later. Same-
sex marriages performed before Proposition 8 was passed will
remain valid, but same sex marriages are no longer performed in
California.

Homosexuality and Legal Rights

Can you imagine if the voting rights of black Americans, a right granted to them by the Supreme Court
of the United States, could be taken away if a majority of white people voted on it? Or what if all the

What's That Mean?

Perception is the way a person looks at and understands a situation.

Status is the position of something in comparison to something else.

blondes and brunettes in the world could vote that red-haired people not be allowed to get married and have children? Can you imagine what it would be like to have *your* rights taken away by a majority vote?

One of the reasons why gay people have had to fight so hard for "equal protection under the law" may be the **perception** of the majority—from the scientific community to the average person—of the gay community's **status** as a minority group. It seems that the best way for a minority group to be perceived as *deserving* the full rights and privileges enjoyed by the majority is if people are a part of that minority by birth. In other words, through no fault of their own! After all, we don't choose our skin color or our ethnic background.

Children who are born to African American parents can be physically identified as black Americans by the color of their skin, but gay people are a hidden minority. Despite those tired old stereotypes we've talked about, homosexual people cannot be recognized by the way they look or speak or act. They are usually born to "majority" heterosexual parents, and they can either choose to identify themselves

Lt. Dan Choi, an officer in the U.S. Army, came out in March 2009 and has become an outspoken opponent of the military's "Don't Ask, Don't Tell" policy.

What's That Mean?

When something begins to be taken seriously and has the support of large numbers of people, it is *legitimized*.

as gay to the rest of the world or not as they wish. But if it could be proven that being gay is an inborn genetic or biological trait, the minority status of gay people would be strongly **legitimized**. It is much harder for the straight majority to argue that a law-abiding, tax-paying minority made up of people *born* gay does not deserve their full rights as citizens and fair and equal treatment under the law. Gay rights become, then, a simple matter of fairness!

If being gay is caused by early life experiences and is a psychological rather than a biological trait, even if it's a psychological disorder, gay people's minority status can be compared to other "psychological" minorities (for example, people who suffer from mental conditions like a fear of heights or a desire to wash their hands constantly). Again, in a society that values fairness, it's not legitimate to deny people their rights based on behaviors that do not harm other people and that are private and deeply personal. So, while maybe not quite as strong as the biological argument, a psychological cause for homosexuality still strongly supports gay people's status as a minority group deserving the full legal rights that other minority groups (not to mention the majority) enjoy.

Religion and Homosexuality

The strongest **opponents** of gay rights, religious and political **conservatives**, still argue that being gay is a choice—despite the fact that most of the scientific community and most gay people themselves strongly disagree with them. For many religious conservatives, gay behavior is a serious offense, a sin against God, and the people who engage in these behaviors are sinners. Organized

Some religious groups make their opinion on homosexuality very clear. Many other groups are less obvious but still make LGBT people feel unwelcome. Fortunately, not all religious groups feel the same way.

religious groups continue to actively fight against the rights of gay people at the local, state, and national level. Meanwhile, through the "ex-gay ministries" they support, they continue to subject unhappy, conflicted gay people to psychologically painful and probably useless therapies to change their sexual preference.

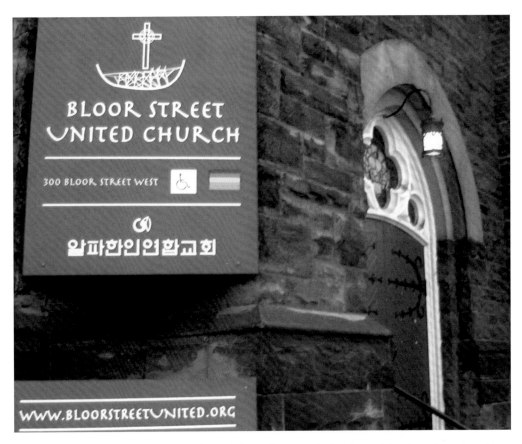

Simply by including the rainbow flag on their sign, this church makes it clear they welcome LGBT people.

EXTRA INFO

The fight for same-sex marriage continues across the country, state-by-state. Progress is being made, despite reversals. According to the National Conference of State Legislatures, here's the status of gay marriage rights in the United States as of April 2010:

- Issues marriage licenses to same-sex couples: *Massachusetts, Connecticut, California*, Iowa, Vermont, New Hampshire, District of Columbia*
- Recognizes same-sex marriages from other states: *Rhode Island, New York, Maryland*
- Allows civil unions, providing state-level spousal rights to same-sex couples: *New Jersey (Note: In Connecticut, Vermont and New Hampshire, same sex marriage has replaced civil unions.)*
- Statewide law provides nearly all state-level spousal rights to unmarried couples (domestic partnerships): *California, Oregon, Nevada, Washington*
- Statewide law provides some state-level spousal rights to unmarried couples (domestic partnerships): *Hawaii, Maine, District of Columbia, Wisconsin*

* The California Supreme Court ruled on May 15, 2008, that same sex couples have the right to marry in California. Proposition 8, which limits marriage to one man and one woman, was passed on November 4, 2008. The decision was appealed. Same-sex marriages performed before Proposition 8 was passed will remain valid, but same sex marriages are no longer performed in California.

The reality of a couple's relationship should not be affected by the opinions of others. Love is love, wherever you find it.

Love

In the end, though, does it really matter what causes homosexuality? Being gay is really all about whom a person loves, isn't it? Even if you don't happen to agree with a person's choice in this most personal and private matter, do you have the right to deny another person's happiness? Does America have the right to deny up to 10 percent of its citizens their full legal and civil rights because the so-called majority doesn't "approve" of their lifestyle?

These may be the real questions to be asking in the twenty-first century. And, as gay people continue to live open, proud, and productive lives and as their straight friends and families continue to learn to understand, love, and respect them for who they are, the future of personal freedom and "the pursuit of happiness" looks brighter for all of us. As the saying goes, "Love conquers all."

Find Out More on the Internet

A Conservative Christian Perspective on Homosexuality
bible.org/article/homosexuality-christian-perspective

Civil Rights and Gay People
www.aclu.org/lgbt-rights

Read More About It

Newton, David E. *Gay and Lesbian Rights: A Reference Handbook.* Santa Barbara, Calif.: Contemporary World Issues, 2009.

Snyder, R. Claire. *Gay Marriage and Democracy: Equality for All.* Lanham, Md.: Rowman & Littlefield Publishers, 2006.

BIBLIOGRAPHY

Abate, Michelle Ann. *Tomboys: A Literary and Cultural History.* Philadelphia, Penn.: Temple University Press, 2008.

BBC Health News Online, June 16, 2008. "Scans See 'Gay Brain Differences'" news.bbc.co.uk/2/hi/health/7456588.stm.

Duberman, Martin. *Cures: A Gay Man's Odyssey, Tenth Anniversary Edition.* Boulder, Col.: Westview Press, 2002.

Johnson, Ramon. *How Many Gay People Are There? Gay Population Statistics.* About.com Guide, gaylife.about.com/od/comingout/a/population.htm

LeVay, Simon. *The Sexual Brain.* Cambridge, Mass.: MIT Press, 1994.

Newton, David E. *Gay and Lesbian Rights: A Reference Handbook.* Santa Barbara, Calif.: Contemporary World Issues, 2009.

Pascoe, C. J. *Dude, You're A Fag: Masculinity and Sexuality in High School.* Berkeley, Calif.: University of California Press, 2007.

Robinson, T. R. *Genetics for Dummies, Second Edition.* New York: John Wiley & Sons, 2010.

Savin-Williams, Ritch C. *The New Gay Teenager.* Cambridge, Mass.: Harvard University Press, 2005.

Snyder, R. Claire. *Gay Marriage and Democracy: Equality for All.* Lanham, Md.: Rowman & Littlefield Publishers, Inc., 2006.

Swidey, Neil. "What Makes People Gay?" *The Boston Globe.* August 14, 2005.

INDEX

allies 50
American Psychiatric Association (APA) 38, 43

babies 10–12, 14, 18, 21, 30, 33
Bieber, Irving 40
biological sex 11, 16
bisexual 36
brain surgery 36

California Supreme Court 51, 57
celibacy 44
chromosome 11, 25–26
church 36, 44
civil rights 22, 50, 59
conservatives 44, 55

depression 44
Diagnostic and Statistical Manual of Mental Disorders (DSM), 38, 43
Duberman, Martin 37, 48, 61

effeminate 46
electroshock 36

Freud, Sigmund 36

gay liberation movement 38
gender 11–16, 18–22, 39, 43–44, 46–48

gender identity 16, 18, 22, 39, 48
gender roles 14, 16, 22, 43, 46–47
transgender 16, 18, 20–21
Gender Disorder in Childhood 43
gene 24–27, 29
genetics 24, 34, 49, 61
genitalia 11, 18

hormone 18, 29, 33, 36
Human Rights Campaign 16

intersex 18

lesbian 27, 30, 32–33, 36, 38, 46, 60–61

mental health 38, 43–44, 48
military 18, 51

oppression 36, 51

penguin 30
pregnancy 29, 33
prejudice 36
prenatal 29
Proposition 8 57
psychologist 27, 35–36

religion 55
reparative therapy 38, 44

sexuality 9, 23, 61
   heterosexuality 30, 50
   homosexuality 9, 21,
   26–27, 29–30, 33, 35–36,
   38–40, 42–43, 47–50, 54,
   59
sexual orientation 21, 26, 36,
39, 44, 47, 49
sexual re–assignment surgery
19

sexual reproduction 12–14, 24
sissies 13, 43
sperm 11–12, 25–26
stereotype 39, 46–47, 52

tomboy 13, 23, 43, 46, 61
twin 25–27, 29, 33–34
   twin studies 27, 33–34

ultrasound 11

ABOUT THE AUTHOR AND THE CONSULTANT

Bill Palmer has been involved in LGBT issues since he was coordinator of his university's gay student alliance in the late 1970s. He also worked for many years for one of the largest academic publishers of LGBT books and journals in the world. Bill lives with his partner of thirty-plus years in Upstate New York.

James T. Sears specializes in research in lesbian, gay, bisexual, and transgender issues in education, curriculum studies, and queer history. His scholarship has appeared in a variety of peer-reviewed journals and he is the author or editor of twenty books and is the Editor of the Journal of LGBT Youth. Dr. Sears has taught curriculum, research, and LGBT-themed courses in the departments of education, sociology, women's studies, and the honors college at several universities, including: Trinity University, Indiana University, Harvard University, Penn State University, the College of Charleston, and the University of South Carolina. He has also been a Research Fellow at Center for Feminist Studies at the University of Southern California, a Fulbright Senior Research Southeast Asia Scholar on sexuality and culture, a Research Fellow at the University of Queensland, a consultant for the J. Paul Getty Center for Education and the Arts, and a Visiting Research Lecturer in Brazil. He lectures throughout the world.